Living in a Biome

Life in a Wetland

by Carol K. Lindeen

Consulting Editor: Gail Saunders-Smith, Ph.D.

Consultant: Sandra Mather, Professor Emerita
Department of Geology and Astronomy, West Chester University
West Chester, Pennsylvania

Capstone
press

Mankato, Minnesota

Pebble Plus is published by Capstone Press
151 Good Counsel Drive, P.O. Box 669, Mankato, Minnesota 56002
http://www.capstonepress.com

1 2 3 4 5 6 08 07 06 05 04 03

Library of Congress Cataloging-in-Publication Data
Lindeen, Carol K., 1976–
   Life in a wetland / by Carol K. Lindeen.
   p. cm.—(Pebble plus: Living in a biome)
   Summary: Simple text and photographs introduce the wetland biome,
including the environment, animals, and plants.
   Includes bibliographical references (p. 23) and index.
   ISBN 0-7368-3405-2 (softcover) ISBN 0-7368-2104-X (hardcover)
   1. Wetland animals—Juvenile literature. 2. Wetland plants—Juvenile literature.
[1. Wetland animals. 2. Wetland plants.] I. Title. II. Series.
QH87.3 .L54 2004
578.768—dc21   2002155684

Editorial Credits
Martha E. H. Rustad, editor; Kia Adams, designer and illustrator; Juliette Peters, cover production designer; Kelly Garvin, photo researcher;
   Eric Kudalis, product planning editor

Photo Credits
Ann & Rob Simpson, 8–9
Bruce Coleman Inc./C. C. Lockwood, 4–5, 14–15
Corbis, 1
PhotoDisc, Inc./6–7
Robert McCaw, 18–19, 20–21
Tom & Pat Leeson, 10–11
Tom Stack & Associates/Peter Mead, cover; Dawn Hire, 12–13; Doug Sokell, 16–17

Note to Parents and Teachers

The Living in a Biome series supports national science standards related to life science. This book describes and illustrates animal and plant life in wetlands. The photographs support early readers in understanding the text. This book also introduces early readers to subject-specific vocabulary words, which are defined in the Glossary section. Early readers may need assistance to read some words and to use the Table of Contents, Glossary, Read More, Internet Sites, and Index/Word List sections of the book.

Word Count: 140
Early-Intervention Level: 13

Table of Contents

What Are Wetlands?

A wetland is an area of
land covered by water.
Marshes and swamps
are wetlands.

Wetlands are found in many parts of the world. Wetlands are often near oceans, lakes, and rivers.

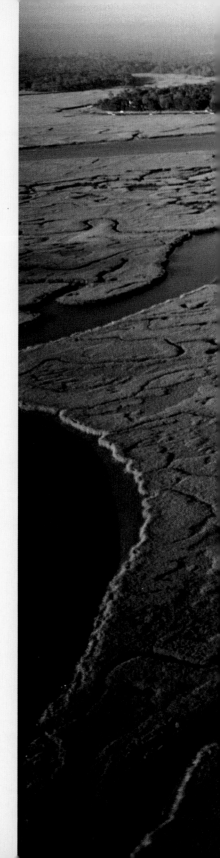

Major wetlands

Wetland Animals

Snails crawl on plants and
on wet ground in wetlands.
Snails carry shells on
their backs.

Cranes are tall birds with long legs. Cranes wade in the water. They eat fish.

Alligators live in some
wetlands. They crawl on land
and swim in shallow water.
They eat fish, frogs, and
other small animals.

Wetland Plants

Many types of trees grow in wetlands. Bald cypress trees have tall trunks.

Reeds grow in the water
in wetlands. Reeds are tall,
hollow grasses.

Moss grows on logs, rocks, and wet shores in wetlands.

Living Together

Many animals find food in wetlands. Plants grow well in the water and wet ground. Wetlands are full of life.

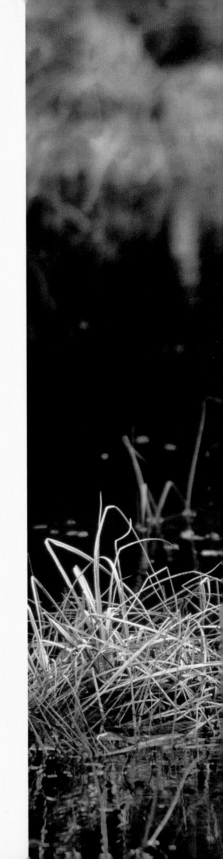

Glossary

hollow—to have empty space inside

lake—a large body of water with land on all sides

marsh—an area of land that is wet; trees and other plants grow in marshes.

moss—a soft, short plant with no roots; moss grows on damp soil, rocks, and tree trunks.

shallow—not deep

shell—a hard outer covering; snails have hard shells; shells protect snails and give them shelter.

shore—the land along the edge of a body of water

swamp—an area of low, wet land where plants grow in the water

wade—to walk in shallow water

Read More

Bishop, Amanda, and Bobbie Kalman. *What Are Wetlands?* Science of Living Things. New York: Crabtree, 2003.

Gray, Shirley. *Wetlands.* First Reports. Minneapolis: Compass Point Books, 2001.

Richardson, Adele D. *Wetlands.* The Bridgestone Science Library. Mankato, Minn.: Bridgestone Books, 2001.

Internet Sites

Do you want to find out more about wetlands?
Let FactHound, our fact-finding hound dog, do the research for you.

Here's how:

1) Visit *http://www.facthound.com*

2) Type in the **Book ID** number: **073682104X**

3) Click on **FETCH IT**.

FactHound will fetch Internet sites picked by our editors just for you!

Index/Word List